To

From

Poems For The Little Ones

And The Big Ones Too!

Pierre D. Perry

Poems For The Little Ones

And The Big Ones Too!

PDP
Publishing

Henderson, North Carolina

Published by PDP Publishing
1725 Graham Avenue
Henderson, North Carolina 27536

First Printing

A trademark design belonging to PDP
Publishing and Pierre D. Perry

Cover design by Pierre D. Perry

Poem on back cover: "Playground Fun" written by Pierre D. Perry

ISBN-13:978-1-6866-9412-7

Printed in the United States of America

Acknowledgments

First of all, I would like to thank God for His everlasting love. For I know that without Him, none of this is possible.

I would like thank my daughters, Cierra and Kenya, for being such great daughters and inspiration.I want to thank them for putting up with me, and for giving me material to use in my writing.

I would like to thank my mother, Mrs. Phylis R. Perry, for encouraging me to write, and for just being a great mother.

I would like to thank my grandson, Tre Boston Jr., for being my inspiration for completing this book.

I would also like thank everyone and anyone who has ever given me a word of encouragement, or have supported me in any kind of way.

And thank you to all the teachers out there who are providing our children with the best education possible. Keep doing what you're doing, because we need you.

Dedicated to my grandson,

Tre Boston, Jr.

Enjoy being a kid for as long as you can

Table of Contents

Fun Times (Part One)

Bed Time (Part Two)

Childhood Years (Part Three)

The Learning Stage (Part Four)

Inspirational (Part Five)

A Funny Thing Happened (Part Six)

A Message to the Parents

Greetings to all and thank you for taking time to read or share with your child, my work. It is truly an honor and a pleasure to have you choose my book.

Over the years I have written over twenty-five books. This is my first book of children poems to be published. I've been sitting on this book for a very long time. Some of these poems have been written years ago. I wanted to wait until I could get an illustrator to illustrate my book before publishing these poems, but that hasn't worked out for me. Therefore, I decided to go ahead and published the book without illustration (believe me, I know it would be a lot better with pictures for the kids).

The age range for the poems in this book varies. Some of the poems are for very young children who will need them read to them, while others could be read by older kids. I'm not putting an age range for this book because it depends on the individual child's ability to read and comprehend as to whether a poem is for them or not. I do believe some of the poems are more suitable for more advanced children, while some are to be read by the parent. I tried to keep the poems as basic and simple as possible for the reader who is just beginning. I do believe this book is a great tool for parents who are trying to teach their children how to read, while introducing them to poetry. The poems in this book should be very relate-able for most children.

Once again, thank you for your time, and please enjoy the time you have to spend with your child or children. I hope my book helps to make it just a little more easier for you to do so.

Pierre D. Perry

Poems For the Little Ones

Part One
FUN TIMES

Let's Have Some Fun!

When the sun is shining
All nice and bright,
Right away I know
My day will be alright.

I'm always happy
To see the beautiful sun.
It lets me know
It's time to have some fun.

No video games,
Nor watching T.V.
Playing outside
Is where I want to be.

Let's have a good time
On this beautiful day!
Let's all go outside
And have fun and play!

Playground Fun

We go from side to side!
We go around and around!
We have so much fun
On the playground!

We go down the slide,
And across the bars.
We swing so high,
We can touch the stars.

We hop! We skip!
We run! We jump!
Sometimes we fall
On our rumps.

There are great big smiles
On every face.
The playground is
Our favorite place!

I Can Ride My Bike!

I can do it! I can do it!
I can ride my bike!
Now I can ride
Wherever I like!

I can ride my bike
To the neighborhood park!
I can ride my bike
Until it gets dark!

I can ride my bike
With my mother!
I can ride my bike
With my big brother!

I can ride my bike
Out in the sun!
Riding my bike
Is soooo much fun!

Things I Like To Do

Running, Jumping,
And riding my bike.
These are some of the things
That I like.

I like camping, swimming,
And fishing too.
There are so many things
I like to do.

I like reading, writing,
And watching T.V.
Playing video games
Is fun to me.

I like singing, dancing,
And playing sports too.
These are just a few things
I like to do!

My Favorite Treat

When I'm down and out,
And feeling bummy,
Mama gives me something
Yummy to my tummy.

It's smooth and creamy,
And cold as ice.
But when it's in my mouth,
It tastes so nice.

Chocolate is good,
And so is cherry.
Vanilla is great,
But I love strawberry.

Cakes are delicious,
And pies are sweet.
But ice cream is
My favorite treat!

Summertime! Summertime!

Summertime! Summertime!
Summertime is here!
Summertime! Summertime!
The best time of the year!

School is out!
Summer vacation!
No homework,
Just relaxation!

Playing at the beach,
And laying in the sun!
Summertime! Summertime!
Fun! Fun! Fun!

Hotdogs, hamburgers
At a family cookout.
Good times are
What summer is all about!

RaiNy Day

Rain has been falling
All during the day.
I wish this rain
Would just go away.

I know we need rain
For the flowers to grow.
But I wish this rain
Would hurry up and go.

I'm stuck inside,
And can't go out to play.
I wish this rain
Would just go away!

But on-the-other-hand,
There's no need to complain.
I'll just go outside
And play in the rain.

My FrieNd aNd I

My friend and I
Walk hand in hand,
Laughing and giggling,
While walking in the sand.

We sing and dance,
My friend and I.
We like to pretend
That we can fly.

We hop, skip,
And sometimes run.
My friend and I
Have so much fun.

I love my friend,
That I won't deny.
No one can come between
My friend and I.

My Buddy

My Buddy is my dog,
And my dog's name is Ice.
I love my Buddy,
Because he's so nice.

My Buddy likes to bark,
And he also likes to eat.
He really gets excited
When he gets a doggie treat.

My Buddy likes to run,
And he also likes to play.
He jumps all over me
Whenever I've been away.

My Buddy is a good dog,
And he's my best friend.
I will always love my Buddy,
Until the very end.

BasketbaLL JuNKy

I'm a basketball junky,
And I'll tell you why.
Nobody loves basketball
More than I.

Winter, spring,
Summer or fall.
Anytime of the year,
I love playing basketball.

I love to play basketball
With my friends in the park.
I will play basketball
Outside in the dark.

I have so much fun
On the basketball court.
That's why basketball
Is my favorite sport.

part two

Bed Time

Goodnight Sweetheart

Goodnight sweetheart,
Lay your head to rest.
Pleasant dreams my dear child,
I wish you the best.

Goodnight sweetheart,
Please don't shed a tear.
Close your eyes,
You have nothing to fear.

Goodnight sweetheart,
This will always hold true...
God loves you,
And I do too!

Time For Bed

Nighttime has come,
And it's time for bed.
No more playing around,
It's time to rest my head.

I must brush my teeth,
And say good night.
No need to fret,
Nor put up a fight.

The moon is out,
It's dark outside,
And if I don't get to bed,
Mama will tan my hide.

Sweet Dreams

Sleep well little one,
And may your dreams be sweet,
Just like the food
You love to eat.

Sweet dreams little one,
Go ahead and dream away.
Dream of yourself
Having fun at play.

Sweet dreams! Sweet dreams!
Get you plenty of rest,
So that you may awaken,
And be at your best.

WHiLe YoU SLeep

While you sleep,
God watches over you.
He sees every breathe you take,
And everything you do.

He watches your little hands,
And your little feet.
He listens to the sound
Of your precious heartbeat.

He never says a word,
Not one little peep.
He just watches over you
While you sleep.

Nighttime Prayer

As I lay me down to sleep,
I pray to God,
My soul You'll keep.

Keep me safe
From all danger and harm.
Hold me close
In Your loving arms.

Thank You, God,
For all that You do.
I know that You love me,
And I love You, too!

Amen

Bedtime Story

Please! Please!
Tell just one more!
Tell me a bedtime story
That makes my mind soar.

Take me to a wonderland,
Or some magical place.
Tell me a story
About far in outer space.

I wanna hear all about
Beautiful queens and kings.
Please tell me a story
About exciting things.

Please! Please!
One more for the night.
But just not a story
Of horror and fright!

When Mommy Tucks Me In

I love when mommy
Tucks me in at night.
She always makes sure
I'm in nice and tight.

She fluffs my pillow
Just right for my head,
And makes sure I'm comfortable,
All snug in my bed.

She says a little prayer,
Then not another peep.
She kisses me goodnight,
And I'm off to sleep.

WHeN Daddy SiNgS

When daddy sings
To me at night,
I know he thinks
He's doing what's right.

He tries so hard
To sing my favorite song,
But daddy's singing
Is just all wrong.

When daddy sings,
He gives it his best.
But I wish he'd be quiet
And give it a rest.

But that's alright,
And that's okay.
I still love my daddy,
Anyway.

Mama Knows Best

I wanna grow up
To be big and strong.
I must drink plenty of milk,
And sleep all night long.

I wanna grow to be tall,
As tall as can be.
I wanna be big and tall
Just like the oak tree.

Mama says
I must get lots of rest,
So I'm off to sleep,
Because mama knows best!

Good Night!

Good night my child,
Rest your little head.
Good night sweet child,
Enjoy your nice warm bed.

Good night precious child,
Sweet dreams to you.
Good night lovely child,
May all your dreams come true.

Good night blessed child,
Sleep well and sleep tight.
Good night my child,
Please have a good night.

Part Three
CHildHood Years

FuN at tHe Zoo

For the first time
I visited the zoo.
I saw a lion, a tiger,
And a monkey too.

I saw all kinds of animals
At the zoo today.
I saw a baby elephant
Playing in the hay.

I saw a tall giraffe
With a very long neck.
And some funny looking bird
Gave me a soft peck.

I saw a little bear,
And a big bear too.
I had so much fun
On my visit to the zoo.

Big Airplane

Big airplane
High up in the sky,
Everyday I watch
As you fly by.

Big airplane
Always on the go.
Where are you going?
I want to know.

Big airplane
High above my head.
You're so loud,
I can't hear what I said.

Big airplane
With your wings so wide,
Could you please
Take me for a ride?

FiSHy! FiSHy!

Fishy! Fishy!
In the water so blue,
Oh, how I would love
To swim with you!

Fishy! Fishy!
Swimming in the sea,
Please slow down
And wait for me.

Fishy! Fishy!
In the water so deep.
I promise to be quiet,
Not one little peep.

Fishy! Fishy!
Please don't swim away.
I just want to
Come in and play.

The Fair Is Coming!

The fair is coming! The fair is coming!
The fair is coming to town!
Cotton candy! Candy apples!
And a funny looking clown!

Fun! Fun! Fun!
Everywhere you go.
Games! Food! Prizes!
And even a magic show!

The fair is coming! The fair is coming!
The fair will soon be here!
Oh, how I love the fair!
It's the best time of the year!

Roller coasters, slippery slides,
And a haunted house too!
So many wonderful choices...
Hmmm, what first shall I do?

Lazy Day

Today is a lazy day,
So what can I say?
I'm too lazy
To go out and play.

I'm so lazy,
I can't get out of bed.
So I think I'll stay here
And sleep instead.

I don't want to do anything.
I'm as lazy as can be.
Being this lazy
Really isn't like me.

I will sleep today,
And get plenty of rest.
Tomorrow I hope to be
Back at my very best.

My First Day of School

It's my first day of school,
And I'm as happy as can be.
There's a whole new world
Just waiting on me.

I can't wait to meet my teacher,
And find out her name.
But if it's a man,
I'll be happy just the same.

I'm going to do my very best
Each and every day.
I will be good in school,
And do what the teacher says.

Learning new things
Is so very cool.
That's why I'm so happy
It's my first day of school!

My Best Friend

I have a best friend
Who is very nice to me.
We laugh and play together,
And we're as happy as can be.

We get along great
While playing in the park.
We both have dogs
Who really like to bark.

We're both the same age,
And we like the same game.
And the scary thing is
We both have the same name.

I love my best friend,
He's as great as can be!
So, I guess y'all have figured,
My best friend is me!

Me and Baby Brother

Me and baby brother
Were playing on the bed.
Baby brother fell off
And bumped his head.
Mama rushed in,
And then she said,
"No more playing with baby brother
on the bed."

Strange Sound

Last night while I was sleeping,
I heard a strange sound.
So I thought I'd get up
And take a look around.

I looked under my bed,
But nothing was there.
I looked and I looked,
I couldn't find it anywhere!

So I went back to bed,
And there was the sound.
Once again I got up,
And took a look around.

I heard the sound coming
From the room next door.
It was just my daddy.
Loudly, he snores.

My New Baby Brother

He's kind of short,
Which means he's not very tall.
He's not very big,
Which means he's kind of small.

Though he can't talk,
He has a lot to say.
And though he can't walk,
He can still crawl away.

He's my baby brother,
And he's depending on me,
To be the best big brother
I can possibly be.

Part Four

THe LearNiNg Stage

THe ANt CoUNt

1 little ant,
And now there's 2.
3 little ants
Crawling on my shoe.

4 little ants,
5 and 6.
7 little ants
Playing on the sticks.

8 little ants,
One more makes 9.
10 little ants
All marching in a line.

Colors All Around Me

Red is the fire truck
Always on the go.
Black is my cat,
And white is the snow.

A banana is yellow,
And the sky is blue.
Orange is a fruit,
And a color too!

Pink is the dress
Worn by the little girl.
Brown is her hair,
So full of tight curls.

Colors all around me,
And I love them so.
So many beautiful colors
I'm trying to get to know.

BruSHiNg Teeth

I brush my teeth
Before bed at night.
It keeps my teeth
All nice and white.

And then in the morning
When I hit the floor,
I make sure I brush
My teeth once more.

Up and down,
Front and back.
Make sure to floss
Between the cracks.

Brushing my teeth
Is so worth while.
It helps me to keep
My beautiful smile.

CLeaN My RooM

Clean up! Clean up!
It's time to clean my room.
Get up all the trash
With a dust pan and broom.

Gather all my toys,
And put them away.
They will be easy to find
When I comeback to play.

Fold all my clothes,
Put them away nice and neat.
Match all the socks
That goes on my feet.

Make up my bed,
And then I'm done.
In comes mommy,
"Good job, son!"

ANiMaL SoUNdS

Roof, roof, barks the dog,
While the cat says, *meow.*
Quack! Quack! Says the duck,
And *moooo* says the cow.

Cluck goes the chicken.
Oink oink squeals the pig.
Get off my grass!
Screams the old lady in the wig.

ROAR! Goes the lion,
As he makes the ground shake.
A *Hiss* sound is made
By the sneaky little snake.

Ribbit, says the frog
Sitting on the lily pad.
Get those animals out of here!
Yells my dad.

PLay It SaFe

Red means stop,
And green means go.
Yellow means caution,
So move kind of slow.

Look both ways
Before crossing the street.
Make sure its clear
Before moving your feet.

Always wear a seat belt
When riding in a car.
Make sure you have it on,
Regardless of how far.

Sit down in your seat
When on the school bus.
Always play it safe,
And don't make a lot of fuss.

Stranger Danger

A stranger is someone
Whom you don't know.
There will always be strangers
Everywhere you go.

Stay close to your parents
Whenever you're out.
Always pay attention
To your whereabouts.

Never go to a stranger
Just to say hi.
Always make sure your parent
Is standing close by.

If for some reason
You are taken by a stranger,
Yell! Yell! Yell!
Until you are out of danger.

ABC'S

A is for apple.
B is for base.
C is for the cat
My **D**og loves to chase.

E is for elephant.
F is for frog.
G is for the goat
Who eats like a **H**og.

I is for ink.
J is for Jane.
K is for the kid
Who lives down the **L**ane.

M is for Mommy.
N is for not.
O is for the onions
Cooking in the **P**ot.

Q is for quick.
R is for rest.
S is for my sister
Who is taking a Test

U is for umbrella.
V is for vase.
W is for the woman
Having an Xray of her face.

Y is for yes.
Z is for zoo.
You said your ABC's,
And learned some new words too.

A ViSit to tHe PLaNetS

Let's go visit the planets
And have some fun.
We'll learn that planet *earth*
Is the third planet from the sun.

On our visit,
We'll shoot pass the stars.
We'll visit planets: *Venus, Uranus,*
Neptune, Jupiter and *Mars*.

We can't forget about *Saturn,*
That looks like rings around a ball.
And then we'll visit *Mercury,*
The smallest planet of them all.

But before we leave,
There's something we must know,
Where in the world
Did *Pluto* go?

Don't Touch!

When someone says, *don't touch,*
There's nothing more to say.
You should take your hand
And quickly put it away.

Don't ever put your hands
On other people stuff.
If someone says, *Don't touch!*
That should be enough.

Without permission,
Never touch someone's face.
Without permission
Never invade someone's space.

Keeping your hands to yourself
Is not asking too much.
And always remember,
Don't touch means *Don't touch!*

part Five

INSpirationaL

I Can Be

Whatever I want to be,
I can be!
My future in this world
Is totally up to me.

I believe in myself!
I'll always do my best!
I'm just as good
As any of the rest.

I can be a doctor,
A lawyer, or a movie star.
As long as I believe,
I can go very far.

I can be whatever
I choose to be.
Never will I put
A limit on me!

PLay Fair

When playing with others
I will always play fair.
I will be nice
And always share.

I will not be mean
Just to have my way.
I will not be a bully
Whenever I play.

I will always play fair,
I will not cheat.
If I should lose,
I'll accept my defeat.

If I'm at home,
Or in someone else care,
Regardless of where I am,
I will always play fair.

SMiLe!

Smile!
Brighten up your day.
Let your smile
Chase your blues away.

For when you smile,
Your heart fills with joy.
So smile like a kid
With a brand new toy.

Smile with the good,
And smile through the bad.
Let your smile
Keep you from feeling sad.

Greet everyone you meet
With a great big smile.
In the end you will find
It was all worthwhile.

Reading Ralph

Now that Ralph can read,
He thinks it's so much fun.
Learning to read
Is the best thing he's ever done.

Now Little Ralph
Gets a book off the shelf,
And have fun reading
All by himself.

Sometimes Ralph reads
All during the day.
Sometimes he'd rather read
Than go out and play.

Reading is something
Ralph loves to do.
And if he can learn to read,
So can you!

Early Bird Eddie

Early in the morning
Before the break of dawn,
Early Bird Eddie
Is out on the lawn.

Quiet is he,
Not a single peep.
Eddie starts his day
While the other birds sleep.

Early Bird Eddie
Loves to have fun.
But first he believes
In getting his work done.

Just when the other birds
Are starting their day,
Early Bird Eddie
Is already at play.

ANNie tHe ANt

Annie the Ant
Wanted to reach the mountain top.
She kept trying and trying,
And refused to stop.

Though the mountain was big,
And Annie was very small,
She didn't let her size
Keep her from giving her all.

Annie became tired
On the climb along the way.
But she kept on going,
Trying her best every day.

The mountain climb was hard,
But Annie didn't stop.
And before she knew it,
She had reached the top.

Betty tHe BiRd

Betty the Bird
Wanted so badly to fly.
Every day after breakfast,
She would try and try.

She would flap her wings
And jump out of the nest.
Though she didn't get far,
She always gave it her best.

Betty felt sad
Because she could not fly.
Sometimes poor Betty
Would began to cry.

As Betty got older,
She became bigger and stronger.
Now Betty flies high,
And she cries no longer.

Negative Nancy

I don't like your shoes!
I don't like your shirt!
Nancy uses words
That really, really hurt.

You can't do this!
You can't do that!
You're too skinny!
You're too fat!

My soup is hot!
I bet your soup is cold!
My dress is new,
But your dress is old!

Negative Nancy
Never has anything good to say,
So when it comes to playtime,
With her no one will play.

KiNd KeNya

Kenya is very kind
When it comes to others.
She is always nice
To her sisters and brothers.

Kenya lends a helping hand
Whenever she can.
She is always kind
To her fellowman.

Kenya uses kind words like,
Have a good day.
She makes people happy
With the words she says.

Be like Kenya,
And you will find,
You will get along better
When you're nice and kind.

Tammy the Turtle

Tammy the turtle
Wanted to cross the street.
But she was very slow
At moving her feet.

She stuck out her head
To make sure it was clear.
She tried to get across,
And got so so near.

Then came a car
Zooming down the street.
Tammy tucked in her head,
And stopped moving her feet.

With her head in her shell,
Tammy tried to hide.
Then a little girl named Kelsey
Helped her to the other side.

Part Six

A Funny Thing Happened

That's My Silly Kitty

That's my silly kitty
All tangled up in yarn.
Yesterday my silly kitty
Chased a dog from the barn.

Sometimes my silly kitty
Likes to hop around the house.
I've even seen that silly kitty
Eat lunch with a mouse.

Today I saw my silly kitty
Swimming with a fish.
And then I saw that silly kitty
Playing Frisbee with her dish.

I don't understand that silly kitty,
She's a strange one to see.
But still I love my silly kitty,
Because she's purr-fect to me.

There's a Mouse In My House

There's a mouse in my house,
And I want him out!
He's running here! He running there!
He's running all about!

He's beside the stove! He's in my chair!
I saw it run under my bed.
Last night while I was sleeping
It ran across my head.

There's a mouse in my house,
And I don't know what to do.
Today I saw it napping
In my favorite shoe.

I thought I had that mouse,
He was mine at last!
I tried very hard to catch him,
But he was just too fast!

He climbed up the curtain!
He slid down the wall!
He ran around and around,
Until he made me fall.

I got back to my feet
And began to give chase.
But once again it happened,
I fell flat on my face.

I tried to get up,
But I only made it to my knees.
There he was laughing at me,
While eating all my cheese.

To make a long story short,
I'll bring this one to an end.
I can't get rid of that mouse,
So I'll make him my friend.

Something Scary in My Closet

Last night while I was sleeping
I heard a scary sound.
I sat up in my bed
And took a look around.

There was a loud noise
Coming from my closet door.
The sound grew louder,
Like a lion's ROAR!

Was there a lion in my closet?
Or was it a bear?
I became so afraid,
I started pulling my own hair.

Louder and louder
The scary sound became.
And then I heard a scary voice,
Calling out my name.

Mommy! Daddy!
I screamed out each name.
Fast and quickly,
They both came.

As they rushed into my room,
Daddy tuned on the light.
Only to find me
In a terrible state of fright.

I told them both,
There was a monster behind my door.
Daddy said, "Don't worry,
He won't bother you anymore."

"Let's just see what's in your closet,"
Said my mother.
And when she opened the door,
It was just my baby brother.

Lazy Larry

Lazy Larry was so lazy
He never finished anything he started.
Before he would get the to end,
Lazy Larry would depart it.

While saying his ABCs,
Once he got to the letter *C,*
He was too lazy to continue,
So he never made it to letter *D.*

He then started counting to 10,
But when he got to the number 3,
Lazy Larry then said,
"That's enough for me."

While going up stairs,
After taking his first step,
Lazy Larry look back and asked,
"Can I please get some help?"

Lazy Larry started to sneeze,
But he was too lazy to carried through.
When he said, "Aaaah"
He never made it to "Chooo"

Lazy Larry had a long day,
He couldn't stay awake anymore.
He was too lazy to get in bed,
So he went to sleep on the floor.

Aunt Carolyn on the Run

Today I saw aunt Carolyn
Running down the street.
She was running so fast,
Her shoes flew off her feet.

Her dress was blowing
Up in the air.
Her hands were waving
In full despair.

She was huffing and puffing
While running about.
She was gasping for air,
But she didn't give out.

She tripped and fell,
But got back to her feet.
She kept on running
Without missing a beat.

She ran, ran, and ran
Far away from the house,
All because she was afraid
Of a little ole mouse.

Brotherly Love

While my big brother
Was fast asleep,
I snuck into his room
Without making a peep.

As he slept,
I tied his shoe strings together.
I then tickled his nose
With a feather.

He woke up in a hurry,
And tried to give chase.
But luckily for me,
He fail flat on his face.

PiNK Patty at tHe Bat

The score was tied
Eight to eight.
That's when Pink Patty
Stepped up to the plate.

"Pink Patty! Pink Patty!"
The crowd chanted her name.
"One more score
And we're win the game!"

Strike one!
Strike two!
"Pink Patty! Pink Patty!
What are you going to do?"

And then came the pitch,
Right across the plate,
BAM!
Game over...9-8.

In My Attic

In my attic
Lives something very mean.
It has a big ole head,
And walks with a lean.

I tried to pay it a visit,
But it chased me out.
That mean old thing
Had me running all about.

I ducked and dodged
While trying to get through.
Then that mean old thing
Hit me with his shoe.

Never again will I visit,
Because it's mean like no other.
And I don't care
If he is my big brother.

Hide and Seek

Lil Tre and Lil Jay
Were playing outside.
Lil Tre told Lil Jay
It was his time to hide.

Lil Jay ran and hid,
While Lil Tre counted to ten.
But then Lil Tre's mama
Told him to come in.

While Lil Jay was hiding
Up high in a tree,
He thought to himself,
Lil Tre will never find me.

As nighttime came,
And Lil Tre was eating dinner,
Lil Jay was still in the tree
Declaring himself the winner.

The Substitute

When the kids at school
Heard of the substitute today,
They all cheered with joy,
Thinking of how they would play.

When Lil Tre entered the room,
He heard someone call his name.
And when he turned around,
He felt so much shame.

There she stood,
The substitute for the day.
And all Lil Tre could do
Was get on his knees and pray.

He knew today would be
A day like no other,
But little did he know,
The sub would be his mother.

THe ENd

About the Author

Pierre D. Perry is a poet and author of several books in many different genres. He is a U. S. Navy veteran, retired correctional officer, youth basketball coach, and the founder of PDP Publishing. Perry is also the proud father of two beautiful daughters, and a handsome grandson. Perry spends his time coaching and mentoring youth in his community as he tries to make the world a much better place.

Perry currently lives in Henderson, North Carolina, where he is always working on new material.

Henderson, North Carolina

Made in the USA
Columbia, SC
25 March 2020